Greater Than a Tourist – Salt Lake City Utah USA

50 Travel Tips from a Local

Shane A. Reinhard

Shane Reinhard

Order Information: To order this title please email lbrenenc@gmail.com or visit GreaterThanATourist.com. A bulk discount can be provided.

Cover Template Creator: Lisa Rusczyk Ed. D. using Canva.
Cover Creator: Lisa Rusczyk Ed. D.
Image: https://pixabay.com/en/salt-lake-city-utah-capitol-139714/

Lock Haven, PA
All rights reserved.
ISBN: 9781549882005

>TOURIST

Shane Reinhard

BOOK DESCRIPTION

Are you excited about planning your next trip?

Do you want to try something new?

Would you like some guidance from a local?

If you answered yes to any of these questions, then this Greater Than a Tourist book is for you.

Greater Than a Tourist, by Shane A. Reinhard, offers the inside scoop on the area around Salt Lake City, UT. Most travel books tell you how to sightsee. Although there's nothing wrong with that, as a part of the Greater than a Tourist series, this book will give you tips from someone who lives at your next travel destination. In these pages, you'll discover local advice that will help you throughout your trip.

Travel like a local. Slow down and get to know the people and the culture of a place. By the time you finish this book, you will be eager and prepared to travel to your next destination.

Shane Reinhard

TABLE OF CONTENTS

11. Taste Test Utah Breweries

12. Eat Authentic Mexican Food

13. Take A Stroll Down Temple Square

14. Drive Up Big And Little Cottonwood Canyons

15. See The Sights At Red Butte Gardens

16. Plan An Overnight To Mirror Lake

17. Fly Down The Mountain By Zip-Lining

18. Refreshing Water Recreational Activities

19. Catch The Wildlife Up-Close And Personal

20. Get Your Caffeine From Local Coffee Shops and Roasters

21. Chow Down Some Grub At Taggert's

22. Climb Utah's Highest Peaks

23. Cool Off At Timpanogos Cave

24. Stroll Down Historic 25th Street

25. Shopping At City Creek

26. Attend Professional Sporting Events

27. Amateur Sports Can Be Fun, Too

28. Theaters and Music Halls

29. Be Amazed By The Architecture

30. Learn At The Leonardo Museum

31. Enjoy Comedy At The Off-Broadway Theatre

32. Get Painted At Color Runs And Festivals

33. Beat The Heat By Hiking Donut Falls

34. Sleigh Rides In The Winter

35. Find A Local Riverwalk Or Bike Path

36. Dig Away At The Copper Mine

37. Smooth Sailing On The Salt Flats

38. Rendezvous At Roosters

39. Visit The Park City Outlets

40. Movie Locations Filmed In Utah

41. Historical Visit To The Capitol

42. Skating In Circles Inside The Olympic Oval

43. Sundance Film Festival To Witness Celebs, Movies, And More

DEDICATION

This book is dedicated to my wife, Kirsten, who I have enjoyed many opportunities to travel the country with. Here is to many more hikes, strolls, road trips, and airplane rides with you by my side. To my daughter, Lilian, who I hope will one days get to experience the wonders the world has to offer. To my brother, Scott, and sister-in-law, Cindy, whom I have enjoyed road trips with, as we grow our families together. I look forward to great memories to come. To my Mom and Dad, for all the times you took Scott and I across the country in a car, when we were young and impatient, to see the beauty of America. To my late Grandad, Jerry, for taking our family on amazing treks up the Alaskan coast and in the tropical waters of the Bahamas. To the Rocky Mountains, for the heavenliness that I get to witness every morning I awake.

Shane Reinhard

ABOUT THE AUTHOR

Shane Reinhard is a teacher who lives in Riverdale, UT with his

wife, their daughter, and their yellow lab, Minne. He loves

teaching and coaching at a local high school in the area. In his

spare time, Shane enjoys sports writing for a local newpaper,

playing his guitar and singing, and fixing up his home.

Shane loves to travel anywhere in the Rocky Mountains, up and

down the coastlines, and backpacking with his hammock if

possible. He has lived in Utah since 1999, and has grown to love

the beauty the state has to offer. From it's sporting events to food

to hiking, Utah has it all.

Shane Reinhard

HOW TO USE THIS BOOK

The Greater Than a Tourist book series was written by someone who has lived in an area for over three months. The goal of this book is to help travelers either dream or experience different locations by providing opinions from a local. The author has made suggestions based on their own experiences. Please do your own research before traveling to the area in case the suggested places are unavailable.

Shane Reinhard

FROM THE PUBLISHER

Traveling can be one of the most important parts of a person's life. The anticipation and memories that you have are some of the best. As a publisher of the Greater Than a Tourist book series, as well as the popular 50 Things to Know book series, we strive to help you learn about new places, spark your imagination, and inspire you. Wherever you are and whatever you do I wish you safe, fun, and inspiring travel.

Lisa Rusczyk Ed. D.

CZYK Publishing

Shane Reinhard

WELCOME TO > TOURIST

Shane Reinhard

INTRODUCTION

"Not all those who wander are lost."

- J.R.R. Tolkien

Traveling is a great way to separate yourself from reality for an extended period of time and see all the things that the world has to offer. When traveling, you can be on a detailed schedule, or just play it by ear. Either way, traveling is something to look forward to.

In this book, you will learn more about Salt Lake City, UT and the surrounding area. The surrounding area of Salt Lake City has a lot to offer visitors. There is something for every kind of traveler, if you like the outdoors or would rather stay inside.

From its elegant mountain range to its storied history from the days of the pioneer, Salt Lake City has grown into a major metropolis with 80% of the population living in the city and in the suburbs. There is plenty to do, and some of the areas you still have to search for, which makes Salt Lake City a mecca for adventure

and excitement.

1. Visit Ski Resorts In The Winter

Salt Lake City prides itself on having the "greatest snow on Earth." While some may debate this point, Utahans agree that there is no better place to ski with resorts less than an hour from the city itself. Many of the resorts were used during the Olympics in 2002, so the slopes continue to be world-class with major ski venues like Park City, Snowbird, Snowbasin, The Canyons, and Deer Valley.

The ski resorts are not only good for their snow. Go up to the top of each mountain to witness the breathtaking scenery, while getting some food and drinks in the process. Also, at Olympic Park, you might be able to catch future Olympians practicing on the ski hill with moguls, jumps, and bobsledding.

2. Don't Just Visit Ski Resorts In The Winter

People may think that ski resorts are only for the winter months, but this could not be further from the truth. Ski resorts are open year-around. In the summer months, many resorts have family-friendly activities which include the alpine slide, trampolines, and much, much more.

If you are around in September and October, you must go to Octoberfest, which is a German festival up at Snowbird. This is authentic German food, beer, music, shopping, and dancing to boot.

Lastly, know that the views from the top of the mountain are just as amazing and a little warmer. But make sure you still bring a jacket as you venture up the mountain. Utahans appreciate the beauty of our state. Get a chance to see the same things we see each and every day.

3. Watch The Sunset From Antelope Island

If you are a fan of sunsets, come check out the ones at Antelope Island. The Island is located just northwest of Salt Lake City, and is a national park surrounded by the Salt Lake. On the Island, there are camping spots, antelope and buffalo sightings, and areas to see the sunsets bounce off the lake into the night. Come see a beautiful array of colors by taking a light hike up to an area of your choice to enjoy the evening. Take a swim right around dusk, as you see the day pass to night.

4. Eat Breakfast At Ruth's

Just east of SLC, up Emigration Canyon, is a wonderful diner named Ruth's. Originally, this historic diner started in a trolley car, and people ventured up the canyon for some great food and an amazing view. Breakfast fans come out of the woodwork to check this restaurant out with fantastic coffee and mammoth biscuits to try. During the warmer months, customers can take the fun outside with live music and brunch options, but get there early, because the diner is not much of a secret anymore, with crowds coming in daily.

Breakfast is not the only thing that makes Ruth's Diner great. If you are of age, there are some great cocktails from a full-service bar that are worth trying. Match your drink with an epic dessert and you will have experienced a full day.

5. Watch The Fireworks On Malan's Peak

Just like in other places across the United States of America, Utah loves its fireworks. But, Utah has most states beat with fireworks on July 4th (Independence Day) and July 24th (Pioneer Day). In Utah, Pioneer Day celebrates the Mormon pioneers that came to live in the area that is now Salt Lake City.

Of course, there are great firework displays across the Valley, but venture up to Ogden, UT, just north of SLC, and hike up Malan's Peak before nightfall. This hike lasts about 2 hours up to an elevation of close to 8,000 feet, where you can gaze at dozens of firework shows all at once. Bring some food and drinks to share, and share the mountain with a few dozen people, while watching the sparks fly. When the fireworks end, camp out on top of the mountain, or take a night hike back down into the Valley.

6. Check Out A Concert At The USANA Amphitheater

The USANA Amphitheater is the biggest outside concert venue in the state of Utah. They offer a wide variety of shows from country, rock, folk, and rap artists, to name a few, from around the globe. Their summer concerts go all the way to October, so they pack in the musical artists that make their way to Salt Lake City. Ticket prices range from about $30 up to premium and VIP seating at about $100 depending on the concert.

Musical artists that have graced this stage include the Scorpions, Imagine Dragons, Luke Bryan, Nelly, and so many more. Enjoy the beautiful outdoor venue with mountains all around. There is not a bad seat in the house.

7. Buy Local At The Salt Lake City Farmer's Market

It is always a great time to buy local food and products at the Downtown Farmer's Market in Salt Lake City. For over 25 years, this tradition has brought in visitors and residents to Pioneer Park summer after summer. Some of the great sells items include fruits and veggies, meats, eggs, and wonderful sauces and spread. All the food is grown right in the state of Utah, as Salt Lake City shows off an assortment of agricultural wealth. Also, look for handmade crafted items from around the state that might look great inside your home. Live entertainment seeps through the market environment with bluegrass, jazz, country, and folk music to get your Saturday started off right.

8. Viewing The Art Scene

Salt Lake City has a vibrant art scene that is valued around the country. Ever 1st Friday of the month, there is a Salt Lake Gallery Stroll to bring business and excitement to businesses and galleries around the city. With over 40 venues to check out, there is plenty of art to go around. This is a free event to the public, which makes for a fun way to meet new people, look over some breathtaking art, and even enjoy snacks that are offered from place to place.

While on a Gallery Stroll, you will be able to meet some of the artists that have worked so hard to get their pieces out to the public. In the end, you have an opportunity to buy their art, or just observe some of the best art in the western United States of the America.

9. Choose From A Variety of Elite Golf Courses

Even though Utah has a winter season, golf courses are still very popular in this desert environment. Golf in Utah can be played generally at the end of March all the way to the end of October. Johnny Miller, a Uniter States (U.S.) Open and Open Championship winner on the Professional Golf Association (PGA) Tour, has designed a few golf courses in the state and none are better than the Stonebridge Golf Club. With 27 championship holes, Miller designed this course to be long and full of water. It is a beautiful layout to witness, but even more beautiful if you are able to handle the challenges the courses has to offer. Other great courses in the Salt Lake City area include Valley View Golf Course, Thanksgiving Point Golf Course, and Bountiful Ridge Golf Course.

10. Hike The Bonneville Shoreline

The Bonneville Shoreline Trail, or the BST, is one of the longest multipurpose trails in the United States of America at over 100 miles. The ultimate goal is for the trail to stretch from central Utah all the way up to the Idaho borderer at almost 300 miles long. The trail was originally created by the ancient lake that covered most of the state of Utah. The lake's remnants left a beautiful trail for people to enjoy. Now, the only lake that is left is the Salt Lake.

Enjoy biking, hiking, walking, bouldering, and much more along this trailhead. Look for beautiful rock formation across the Wasatch Front, as well as rivers and streams that cut across the great landscape at over 5,000 feet of elevation. Be sure to check for markers and signs that may lead you appropriately on the trail. Also, stop the erosion epidemic as people go off the beaten path and cause added destruction to the beauty that the state of Utah holds.

"The world is a book and those who do not travel

read only one page."

- Augustine of Hippo

Shane Reinhard

11. Taste Test Utah Breweries

Many people have the stereotype that Utah does not have good beer because of the religious influence in the state. You may be surprised to know that Utah is quite well-versed in their breweries. When in the Salt Lake Valley, go try some tastings at Epic Brewing, Red Rock Brewing, and Squatters Pub Brewery. There are also a few establishments that allow tours such as Squatters Pub Brewery, Roha Brewery, Epic Brewing, and Wasatch Brewpub.

Also, be sure to head up to Roosters Brewing Company and Restaurant north of Salt Lake City. This family owned business is one of the state's shine gems when it comes to brewing beer.

12. Eat Authentic Mexican Food

Utah has seen a spike in hispanics immigrating into the state. Because of this fact, great Mexican food has also entered the Valley. One of the states best restaurants is the Red Iguana. This establishment is a cozy, fun environment with a varied menu that is catered to an entire family. Try great entrees, drinks, and desserts. The enchilada sauce is something you should get on every main course with its unique flavoring.

Javier's Authentic Mexican Food has locations in northern Utah, and they provide a massive amount of food for you to enjoy. With seven locations to choose from, Javier's family business has grown into a Utah staple.

Other Mexican restaurants in the Salt Lake area include Maria's Mexican Restaurant, Beto's, and, if you want something quick, try Cafe Rio.

13. Take A Stroll Down Temple Square

Temple Square is one of the most beautiful destinations in downtown Salt Lake City. The location is not just about the Mormons in the area, but shares much more about the state's history with beautiful architecture and wonderful dining to match. In terms of history, Temple Square have close to 20 buildings to visit that embody the architecture and appeal of the Beehive State. Architecture like this is very rare at this point across the United States of America.

In the summer, you can head down to Temple Square to witness the creative fountains and gardens that line the landscape of this venue. In the winter, Temple Square is covered in lights at they celebrate the holiday season. There is never a bad time to go down to Temple Square for a stroll.

14. Drive Up Big And Little Cottonwood Canyons

While in Utah, you have to go up Big and Little Cottonwood Canyons. They are both less than 30 minutes from the Salt Lake City Airport, and you will be able to observe brilliant scenic views of some of the best nature around. With ski resorts, hiking trails, camping grounds, and rock climbing routes, there is plenty for you to take in on your journey up the mountain.

The Big Cottonwood Canyon has two amazing resorts which include Brighton and Solitude only 15 miles up the canyon. They both have year round events that you can partake in. Bring your own food or get a meal up on the mountain. If you are down for some hikes, travel up to Dog Lake, Desolation Lake, or Silver Lake for the day or overnight by bringing your backpack up.

The Little Cottonwood Canyon is equally impressive,

but only seven miles up the hill. Snowbird and Alta ski resorts are embedded in this canyon. Alta is one of the few resorts left in the United States of America that is only available for skiers and not snowboarders. At Snowbird, try their Mexican restaurant, *La Caille,* which serves up magnificent courses and tasty drinks.

The granite that you see within this canyon was the same granite used to build the Salt Lake Temple in Temple Square. Aligned with pine trees and running streams, this canyon remains one of the beautiful locations in the state of Utah.

15. See The Sights At Red Butte Gardens

The Red Butte Garden, on the campus of the University of Utah, is much more than just a garden, but let's start there. With displays and collections ranging from conifer, rose, daffodil, and ornamental grass, there is quite the variety at Red Butte Gardens. Other than their garden, these gardens have a lovely amphitheater that houses their outdoor concert series. But, do check the weather because, rain or shine, they will house a concert. So, make sure to dress in the right attire for the evening.

Other events at Red Butte Gardens include "Poetry In The Garden," and workshops for children and adults. In an academic setting, teachers and students can get into the action to for educational purposes.

16. Plan An Overnight To Mirror Lake

One of the best overnight trips is going up to the Mirror Lake. This location can be reached by driving east of Salt Lake City, but its value is worth the trip. On your way, look for wildlife, stop at the local "Mirror Lake Diner," and check out Provo River Falls. You might even find more than you expected along your journey.

Remember to consider a few things when making your way on this trek. First, you should be prepared and plan accordingly so you set yourself up for success. Know what to do if weather strikes, and have a map in case you get lost out in the wilderness. Secondly, find solid places to camp. Be a couple hundred feet away from any water source and walk on trails to limit erosion. At all times, respect the wildlife that you see, and keep your food tucked away from these critters. Lastly, keep your campfires small, so they resemble little impact after usage. All of these tips will save you and the environment.

17. Fly Down The Mountain By Zip-Lining

A great way to get outdoors in the state of Utah is to go out and zip-line. This activity is one where you can see the beautiful scenery around you, while racing down to the landing deck. Some zip-lining establishments have one long zip-line where you descend to the final landing desk, or others allow you to zigzag your way down the mountain, stopping at different decks along the way.

Snowbird Ski Resort offers a zip-line in the summer that travels 1,000 feet. Another zip-line business you may want to check out is the MAX Zip Line, which is just south of Salt Lake City. Weave your way down a variety of platforms to stop and stare at the magnificence around you.

18. Refreshing Water Recreational Activities

Water recreation around Salt Lake City is a necessity when you are in the state. From water-skiing, fishing, boating, swimming, rafting, and kayaking, there is something for everyone here.

If you enjoy some of these activities, attempt to spend some time at these locations: Pineview Reservoir, Utah Lake, and Jordanelle State Park. All of these bodies of water have massive space for you to play in or around the water. A small fee will get you into any one of these amazing and relaxing spots. Lay out or play in the friendly waters from dawn until dusk.

19. Catch The Wildlife Up-Close And Personal

There is plenty of wildlife to see in Utah. More than 600 types of birds, reptiles, amphibians, fishes, and mammals call Utah their home. As a wildlife enthusiast, you have the chance to view these creatures up closes, or in some cases, hunt or fish for them. Even though Utah is in a desert, there are wetlands created from the Great Salt Lake. In this habitat, you will be able to witness a plethora of birds, antelope, sheep, deer, and even bison at Antelope Island. Moose can be found up and down Big and Little Cottonwood Canyons.

Remember, if you are interested in hunting or fishing in the Salt Lake area, you will need to receive a license from the Utah Wildlife Resources office. Also, if you would rather not hunt alone, hire an outfitter to take you out hunting to areas that are kept secret.

For those of you who like a contained wildlife environment, hit up Utah's Hogle Zoo, the Tracy Aviary, or Loveland Living Planet Aquarium for more nature fun. These exhibits show off local creatures, as well as some from afar, giving you the full landscape of creation. The zoo has inside and outside exhibits, while the aviary is purely outdoors and the aquarium is an indoor facility.

20. Get Your Caffeine From Local Coffee Shops and Roasters

Coffee is definitely a staple in the Salt Lake Valley. Great shops and roasters reside in the downtown area, and there are plenty to choose from starting with Publik Coffee. They roast their own coffee in Salt Lake City and Park City with space to lounge around. One drink to try is definitely their cold brew, but other recommendations would also come off their food menu, like their breakfast toast.

The next day, in the Salt Lake area, get your coffee from Alchemy Coffee. They are starting to make the rounds in the Valley with three separate locations across the Wasatch Front. Currently, they use another's coffee beans (Salt Lake Roasting Company whom we will talk about next), but they are on their way to roasting themselves, too. Do yourself a favor and order a flat white, and your eyes will be opened.

Lastly, the Salt Lake Roasting Company should be on your coffee list before you go. A staple in Salt Lake for over 30 years, you should get yourself a pastry and order a Banana Mocha Frappacino. Then, walk up their staircase to a seating area that oversees the city.

Shane Reinhard

"The journey of a thousand miles begins with a

single step."

- Lao Tzu

Shane Reinhard

21. Chow Down Some Grub At Taggert's

If you are looking for a family owned and a family friendly restaurant, Taggert's Grill is for you. Taggert's is really off the beaten path, northeast of Salt Lake City, off of I-84, but well worth the travel. Located right in the heart of Morgan canyon, Taggert's has the view and the food all under control. Their menu offers mouth-watering sandwiches and burgers, with homemade desserts to top off your meal.

On the back patio, Taggert's has luscious foliage, elegant peacocks, and a waterfall pond all to gaze at. Take a deep breathe and find your happy place at Taggert's Grill.

After you get a bite to eat, take a tube or a raft down the Weber River. This river is family friendly for all ages. Barefoot Tubing is a tubing rental and shuttle service for you to ride down the river safely, while still having a lot of fun. If you want to try some rafting, enter into a half-day trip that lasts up to 2 hours. Or you can add a mountain bike ride to travel by land, as well as water on your trip.

22. Climb Utah's Highest Peaks

Because Utah is located along the Rocky Mountains, you bet there are some great mountains to scale. The tallest peak in Utah is King's Peak at an elevation of 13,528 feet. Other peaks that follow in the King's Peak shadow include Mt. Peale (12,721 feet), Mount Timpanogos (11,750 feet), and Mount Ellen (11,522 feet). These are all considered prominence peaks, which are all over 2,000 feet of elevational climb. There are over 80 peaks in the state of Utah that all have prominence peaks over 2,000 feet. Pick your peak and hike to the top. Currently, less than 10 individuals have climbed 80 or more peaks in the state of Utah. Maybe you can shoot to be in this rarified air, too.

23. Cool Off At Timpanogos Cave

Spend time traveling just south of Salt Lake City to American Fork to the Timpanogos Cave. The cave shows the beauty of nature underground. Rangers, that are on staff, will guide your though the caverns, as they share about the magnificent formations. Experience what Timpanogos Cave has to offer with a visitors center, a cave, and a paved trail leading up to the top. In the summer, be sure to stay hydrated because the pavement can get up to 100 degree Fahrenheit because the pathway is a mile and a half long. Also, do not wear any clothing, gear, or shoes that have been in a cave before. This is to prevent the White-nose Syndrome, which is killing bats by the millions in North America.

If you choose, you can do a caving tour, where you actually rope down the Hansen cave for a tour that lasts for an hour and half. This is the same hike, as the original explorer Martin Hansen achieved right before the 20th century. No more than five people can participate in the exploration at a time, so get yourself scheduled today.

24. Stroll Down Historic 25th Street

This historic street, located in the heart of Ogden, UT, just north of Salt Lake City, has a storied history. Originally, the railroad met in Ogden around 1869, which started to grow the city substantially. At one time, this street was dangerous, with drug dealers, brothels, and gangs that roamed the streets. Today, Historic 25th Street, or H25, is a lot more enjoyable with food, drinks, art, and shopping with every step you take. More than one million people visit the H25 every year.

Community Partners like Coca-Cola, American First Credit Union, and R.A.M.P. add to Historic 25th Street's appeal and recreation. Are you a brunch kind of person? Consider Pig In A Jelly Jar for some fun menu items. Wanting dinner? Visit the Hearth on 25th Street for a wonderful sit-down evening with great courses and wine selections. Then, peruse through shops and local art dealers. If you like ethnic food, spend some time at Tona Sushi or World's Greatest Pho.

25. Shopping At City Creek

City Creek, located in downtown Salt Lake City, is the pinnacle of malls in the state of Utah. You can experience it all at City Creek Center. There are stores, dining, events, and so much more. With over 100 restaurants and stores to choose from, everyone will find something to do.

Try getting some lunch at Blue Lemon, which offers fresh and delicious items. Next, grab a cup of tea at Teavanna, while you visit elite stores such as Porsche Design, Michael Kors, Nordstrom, West Elm, and many more. Finish up your evening by getting some dinner and dessert at the Cheesecake Factory.

Year-around, you can participate in three events at the City Creek Center. First, feed the fish every Saturday morning at 10 a.m. at their local pond full of trout. Next, take a tour of the architecture at City Creek Center by heading over to the sky pedestrian bridge where you can look out to view the sky and all its wonders. Lastly, American First Credit Union puts on a fountain show every hour for the public to see. You can choose to get wet from the water if you are looking for a way to beat the heat.

26. Attend Professional Sporting Events

Utah sports may not be as big as some of the cities across the nation, but fans are proud of their teams nonetheless. The Utah Jazz are well-established in Salt Lake City, and will have a renovated arena for the upcoming season, after coming off a year where they made it to the playoffs. Major League Soccer also has a team in Utah. Real Salt Lake plays at Rio Tinto Stadium, where close to 20,000 fans band together to root on the Claret and Cobalt, who won a championship in 2009. Parking can be expensive at these kind of sporting events. But, there are some surrounding neighborhoods where, if you are willing to walk, you can save yourself some money while getting some exercise in the process. No matter your sport, there is something for any fan from Utah or outside the state.

27. Amateur Sports Can Be Fun, Too

Professional teams are not the only sporting events in the Salt Lake area. Major universities like the University of Utah and Brigham Young University have impressive football and basketball teams, while being connected with sports in the Pac-12 conference and the West Coast Conference, which are major players in the college athletic landscape.

Salt Lake City also have a few minor league sport teams like the Salt Lake Bees, which are a baseball farm team for the Los Angeles Angels, and the Utah Grizzlies, which are an affiliate of the Anaheim Ducks. Come see players that may be the future of their respective organizations.

28. Theaters and Music Halls

When it comes to the theater and music hall scene, the Salt Lake City area has you covered. Spend a night at Capitol Theatre which house events from the Utah Opera, Ballet West, and the Woodbury Dance Company. The acts at this venue are world-class.

Pioneer Theatre is another option to consider. This theatre is connected with the University of Utah, and houses close to 10 plays every single season. Go check out their intimate playhouse.

If you enjoy music halls, Kingsbury Hall on the campus of the University of Utah is for you. 16 performances happen at this venue yearly, and over half of them are family friendly. One of their premiere events every October is Thriller with a variety of music including Michael Jackson's work of art.

29. Be Amazed By The Architecture

Salt Lake City has some awe-inspiring architecture in the heart of downtown. First off, the Salt Lake City Library was designed by the great Moshe Sadie, so take a look at the architecture, and then go in and read a book that connects with you. The hope of this architecture piece was to bring about curiosity and imagination for all you grasp its brilliance.

The Cathedral of the Madeleine is the most detailed Catholic Cathedral in the state of Utah. Originally constructed in 1900, this building was rededicated in the early 1990s. The cathedral is home to masses, recitals, cultural events, and so much more.

Lastly, if you find old homes enjoyable, travel over to Kearns Mansion off of South Temple. This piece of architecture was built in 1902. You can receive a tour in the months of June, July, August, and during the holiday season in December.

30. Learn At The Leonardo Museum

Open every day of the week, it is always time to learn at the Leonardo Museum. This museum is all about their programs that lead to education for children and adults alike. The cool thing about the Leonardo Museum is it's always changing. So, you could go multiple times throughout the year and see something different.

Every year, the Leonardo has some amazing presentations from mummy exhibits to the Dead Sea Scrolls. Perception: The Illusion Of Reality is one of their staples where they show visitors how amazing the human mind really is.

This museum is family friendly with a studio to get creative through an artistic lens or head over to the Science Lab where you will be able to ask questions about science, while answering your questions through experimentation.

"Wherever you go becomes a part of you

somehow."

- Anita Desal

Shane Reinhard

31. Enjoy Comedy At The Off-Broadway Theatre

Everybody needs a laugh once in a while. That is where Off-Broadway Theatre comes into view in Salt Lake City. For over 20 years, this establishment has made people chuckle, laugh and cry all out of joy.

At the Off-Broadway Theater, you can see parodies, musicals, improvisation, and traditional plays. Year after year, this theatre has some of the best comedians in the state, and some that actually travel outside the state. Each month, come see parody players that fit the theme of each month. Interactive with their actors and actresses, while basking in the atmosphere around you.

32. Get Painted At Color Runs And Festivals

The Color Run is actually a national event that zig-zags across the United States, but they do stop in October in Salt Lake City. The Utah State Fairpark presents this event that is sponsored by the company Lay's. Enjoy running the color run by making your way through a foam zone, inflatable unicorns, and so much more. On top of this, you will get covered in color, so bring clothes you are willing to get messy in.

If you enjoy color festivals, Utah has one of the biggest ones in the western United States at the Sri Sri Radha Krishna Temple in Spanish Fork. For two days a year, mainly over a weekend in March or April, come get colored with your friends and family. This event has live music, dancing, food, and exercise in the form of yoga. Have children in your family? Well, kids are free if they are under the age of 12 years old.

33. Beat The Heat By Hiking Donut Falls

Donut Falls is one of those hike in the Wasatch Front that everyone should do once in their lifetime. This hike is easy in nature, but it still is challenging to a hiker because it is over three and a half miles long out and back. With little to no elevation, the most elevation will be as you climb to the top of the falls. Stay away from morning for this hike, when a ton of people crowd the trails. During the week or each evening is a good time to hike. Families are relatively seen on this hike up to Donut Falls because this experience creates great bonding amongst each other. Hiking in the summer will be a great way to cool off by dunking your head in the falls, or by hiking in the fall, you can bring a hoodie and a warm beverage to keep the hike pleasant.

34. Sleigh Rides In The Winter

Just because carriage rides are banned in Salt Lake City, does not mean that you can't take advantage of sleigh rides outside of the Wasatch Front. Sleigh rides are perfect during the holiday season, or anytime when there is snow on the ground. Up the road, in Park City, All Season Adventures offers dog sledding adventures and sleigh rides with the help of horses. Boulder Mountain Ranch also provides sleigh rides for friends and family up to around six individuals. If you want dinner and a ride, check out The Snowed Inn Sleigh Company at the Park City Mountain Resort.

35. Find A Local Riverwalk Or Bike Path

In the Salt Lake Valley, there are over 150 trails to walk or bike. Ogden, UT offers a River Walk, which is open year around. Start at the Ogden Botanical Gardens, which is the result of a Utah State University Extension Program. Walk east past the George S. Eccles Dinosaur Park up to Rainbow Gardens, which has amazing "Mormon Muffins" at their restaurant, The Greenery, that everyone should try. Stay for dinner as well. The food is superb for a local restaurant in the area. The Ogden River will run beside you the entire time as you take in the sites and sounds.

In terms of biking, there are over 20 cycling trail routes for people to try. Take a ride through the Avenues or up Emigration Canyon. Rides range from intermediate mileage (under 20 miles) well up to highly difficult routes, which are close to 40 milers.

36. Dig Away At The Copper Mine

The Kennecott Copper Mine, owned by the Rio Tinto business group, is one of the most spectacular views to witness in the Salt Lake Valley. This mine is the second largest copper mine in the country. Currently, there are only two manmade objects that can be seen from space: one is the Great Wall of China, and the other is the Copper Mine. Each year, the mine harvests minerals like copper, silver, molybdenum, and gold.

Travel just 28 miles west of Salt Lake City, to see this wonder, which is an open mine that goes down three-quarters of a mile down into the mountainside. Go and learn about the history of mining, in the state, by viewing old artifacts and watching a short film about the production of copper.

As you view the workers in the mine, witness haul trucks that weight over 300 tons, as they drive up and down the mine transporting ore to and fro.

37. Smooth Sailing On The Salt Flats

Over 30,00 acres make up the Bonneville Salt Flats, a few miles west of Salt Lake City. The Salt Flats were formed from the ancient body of water, Lake Bonneville, that used to be in existence. Now, only the Salt Lake remains in its place. As Lake Bonneville shrank, it left salt deposits in the area, where no vegetation can grow. In some areas, there is a marshy environment that allow a habitat for a few animals and plants.

You should visit this area because, even in the summer, the Bonneville Salt Flats looks like they are covered with snow, because of the salt deposits that were left behind. Also, because the area is so flat, the Salt Flats almost allow for the human eye to see the curvature of planet Earth.

38. Rendezvous At Roosters

On Historic 25th Street in Ogden, Roosters Brewing Company and Restaurant was created in 1995. The building where you eat is over 120 years old, and was originally used as a Chinese laundry service as well as a brothel at the turn of the 20th Century. Now, Roosters has 2 locations, including one in Layton, UT.

At the only micro brewery in northern Utah, Roosters offers delicious appetizers and mouth-watering entrees with meal items such as pastas, pizzas, burgers, salads, and sandwiches. If you are interested in a beer, there are 26 options to sort through, but some of their best include the Bees Knees Honey Wheat, Polygamy Pale Ale, and the Two-Bit Ale. They even make homemade root beer and orange cream soda. The environment at this restaurant caters to any walk of live, as all are welcome at this place.

39. Visit The Park City Outlets

When you are in the Park City and you are interested in doing some shopping, head over to the Tanger Outlets. High-end shopping happens here with shops like Abercrombie & Fitch, Coach, and Tommy Hilfiger are reside in one place. You can walk through a variety of stores that sell accessories and jewelry, apparel for adults and children, footwear, specialties, and home furnishings. There are always deals going on at the Tanger Outlets, so check online or at the store to see how you could get the best band for your buck.

Does shopping always make you a little more hungry? There is a Clockwork Cafe to grab a bit to eat, or you check out some sit-down establishments like Café Trio, Loco Lizard Cantina, and The Junction that are nearby.

40. Movie Locations Filmed In Utah

If you are a big movie buff, you may want to visit some areas where major movies were filmed. Robert Redford's 1972 film, "Jeremiah Johnson," was filmed in 100 locations across the state in areas like the Uinta National Forest and the Wasatch-Cache National Forest. Any lovers of the movie "Footloose?" This 1984 gem, with Kevin Bacon, was filmed south of Salt Lake City in American Fork, Lehi, Orem, and Provo. John Cusack starred in the 1985 movie "Better Off Dead," which was filmed at three Utah ski resorts: Alta, Brighton, and Snowbird. "The Sandlot" is one of the most popular movies filmed in the state. Up and down the Wasatch Front, from Ogden to American Fork, "The Sandlot" filmed backyard baseball in the area. Lastly, all three "High School Musical" movies where filmed in Salt Lake City, with East High School getting most of the film time.

"Travel brings power and love back into your life."

- Jalaluddin Rumi

Shane Reinhard

41. Historical Visit To The Capitol

Politics are not just about changing the landscape of the world, but their architecture is also impressive. The Utah State Capitol was finished in 1916 with the help of the same granite used to build the Salt Lake City Temple. With over 50 Corinthian replica columns, this building has a greek-aura about it.

Open weekdays, 9 a.m. to 5 p.m., tours are given every hour to visitors. Things you will learn include Utah's branches of government, facts about the Capitol building, and facts about the state of Utah. You can always bring a picnic to the grounds of the Capitol building. Just clean up after yourself. This is a great activity to bring children and even pets. There is a wonderful trail that goes around the Capitol, so you can see the building from all its many angles.

If you are around in the spring, check out the cherry blossoms. The tress were a gift from Japan to signify friendship after World War II. End of March to the beginning of April is a beautiful time to see these trees showing off.

42. Skating In Circles Inside The Olympic Oval

The Utah Olympic Oval was built int 2002 for the Long Tract Speed Skating events. It is classified as the "Fastest Ice on Earth. This five and a half acre facility offers a wide variety of events and activities for families and friends.

First off, public skating is offered four times a week in the summer months. Glide on the ice in a refreshing environment. Cosmic Skate Night is also a fantastic evening, where the Olympic Oval brings out the state's largest disco ball. Under the black lights, skate the night way with laser lights and a live DJ pumping up the atmosphere. Cosmic Curling is another event where you can learn about this sport with neon lights rocking the joint. Lastly, if you would rather stay off ice, use the running track that encircles the Olympic Oval.

43. Sundance Film Festival To Witness Celebs, Movies, And More

In the month of January, Park City is all about the Sundance Film Festival. Come see movies before they are even out in theaters. Specifically, the Sundance Film Festival puts on The World Cinema competitions. This competition looks to find new films that share voices of people around our world. The hope is for international talent to get recognized for their filmmaking skills. Every year, there is an award ceremony for some of the best dramatic and documentary films at the festival.

Interested in buying tickets for the event? You can purchase individual tickets for less than $30 or you can get a pass for everything that the Sundance Film Festival has to offer for a couple thousand dollars. Either way, you will get to see Utah cinema at a whole new level.

44. Finding Enchanted Ice Castles

The Ice Castles, in Midway, UT, are definitely a sight to see. Bring your significant other or a whole group of friends to take in this brilliant sight. The Ice Castles are lite up with different colors, as you see the beauty that ice holds to the human eye. Over 10,000 icicles are grown and are placed all over the Ice Castle.

Dress like its winter when you come because the Ice Castle is made out of real snow and ice. Even the pathways are made in this way. So, when the weather starts getting cold, think Ice Castles for your next Utah event. The Ice Castles will stay open as long as it stays cold.

45. Lantern Festival In Eagle Mountain

Ever seen the Disney's movie "Tangled?" Remember when the village lifts lanterns up into the night's sky. Well, this can be done in real life at The Lights Festival in Eagle Mountain. In the month of September, spend a magical evening sending lanterns into the sky with hundreds and even thousands of people all at the same time. Kids under 3 years old are free, so take advantage all you young families out there. Each entry receives a lantern, a key chain flashlight, and a marker. This memory will really stick with you for a lifetime.

46. Soar At The Ballon Festival

There are two Ballon Festivals in the state of Utah that you must see to believe. The first is the Ogden Valley Balloon & Artist Festival. In the month of August, head up to Eden, UT to see the balloons flying high in the air. During the weekend, watch as the ballots are launched, live music is played, delicacies for every food lover, and fun games for the family.

Close to Salt Lake City, you can see the Ballon Festival in Sandy, UT. Also, in the month of August, this festival launches balloons at sunrise. In the evening, there is food and entertainment all night long. Hang out with tens of thousands of people, as you enjoy the beautiful color balloons high up in the air.

47. Hanging While Gliding

World-renowned hanging gliding happens in the state of Utah. One of the great locations to paraglide or hang glide is called "The Point." This is located off of the major interstate I-15 between Salt Lake City and Provo. The positive soaring conditions are perfect in this part of the country. There are access roads and buildings for training purposes with hang gliding and paragliding. You must be a member to be involved in this Utah sport, but you can visit the area to watch local paraglider and hang gliders strut their stuff in the air.

48. Trolley Square To-Dos

Since 1908, Trolley Square has been a historical landmark in downtown Salt Lake City. Food and shopping are hot spots on the east side of downtown Salt Lake City. Step into shops like Pottery Barn, lululemon, Alice Lane Home Collection, and so much more.

If you are feeling hungry, walk into The Old Spaghetti Factory for some wonderful Italian food. Enjoy salad, pasta, and an Italian Cream Soda with a glass you actually get to keep. Also, Rodizio Grill is a Brazilian Steakhouse that offers an assortment of food that ranges from common meats, like pork, all the way to exotic ones, like rattlesnake. If you are looking for a meal that is unique, this place is definitely one to look at.

49. 4-Wheeling Somewhere Pretty

Northern Utah has some amazing scenic hotspots when it comes to ATV riding. No matter if you have a Utility side by side, a utility ATV, or four wheelers, there are many places for you to travel in your vehicle. The mass amount of public land makes Utah a great place to find adventure. You might be able to check out land that has been rarely touched. The national forests that surround the state are littered with trails and roads for off-road vehicles. Bountiful Peak, just north of Salt Lake City, is another place to ATV across the state's beautiful landscape. The alpine scenery gives a fantastic view of the Great Salt Lake.

50. More Festivals To Consider

Even though a lot of festivals happening in the state of Utah, there are still so many that have not been mentioned yet. How about the U.S. Open Snowkite Masters? 100 Snowkiters come from around the world to participate in this weekend with events like kite racing, freestyle, and free-riding in Skyline, UT. Any snowboarders or skiers can join for free. Check out this unusual event that is gaining in popularity.

Flower lovers need to go to the Tulip Festival in April. Thanksgiving Point offers this event to the public, where 55 acres of tulip numbering in the hundreds of thousands. Come take a stroll, listen to some music, and buy some goodies by local vendors.

Greek enthusiasts: attend the Annual Greek Festival to experience hospitality as you immerse yourself in a different way of life. For a minimal fee, you can enter into this magnificent weekend in September. Come eat some traditional gyros, baklava, and greek coffee. Enjoy live music, dancing, and bazaar, where you can shop until you drop.

Shane Reinhard

Top Reasons to Book This Trip

- **Mountains**: The scenery is hard to match anywhere else in the world.

- **Recreational Activities**: The world is your oysters with all the extracurriculars you could be a part of.

- **A Family Environment**: Family-friendly attractions are prevalent for any family across the globe.

Shane Reinhard

> **TOURIST**

GREATER THAN A TOURIST

Visit GreaterThanATourist.com
http://GreaterThanATourist.com

Sign up for the Greater Than a Tourist Newsletter
http://eepurl.com/cxspyf

Follow us on Facebook:
https://www.facebook.com/GreaterThanATourist

Follow us on Pinterest:
http://pinterest.com/GreaterThanATourist

Follow us on Instagram:
http://Instagram.com/GreaterThanATourist

Shane Reinhard

> TOURIST

GREATER THAN A TOURIST

Please leave your honest review of this book on Amazon and Goodreads. Thank you.

We appreciate your positive and negative feedback as we try to provide tourist guidance in their next trip from a local.

GREATER THAN A TOURIST

Our Story

Traveling is a passion of the "Greater than a Tourist" series creator. Lisa studied abroad in college, and for their honeymoon Lisa and her husband toured Europe. During her travels to Malta, an older man tried to give her some advice based on his own experience living on the island since he was a young boy. She was not sure if she should talk to the stranger but was interested in his advice. When traveling to some places she was wary to talk to locals because she was afraid that they weren't being genuine. Through her travels, Lisa learned how much locals had to share with tourists. Lisa created the "Greater Than a Tourist" book series to help connect people with locals. A topic that locals are very passionate about sharing.